T0273307

A Dog Day

A Dog Day

or
The Angel in the House

by

Walter Emanuel

Pictured

by

Cecil Aldin

SOUVENIR
PRESS

This edition first published in 2022

This edition first published in 1999 by
Souvenir Press,
an imprint of Profile Books Ltd
29 Cloth Fair
London
EC1A 7JQ
www.souvenirpress.co.uk

First published in Great Britain in 1902 by William Heinemann

1 3 5 7 9 10 8 6 4 2

Printed and bound in Great Britain by TJ Books Ltd, Padstow

A CIP catalogue record for this book is available from the British Library.

ISBN 978 1 80081 026 6

TO
W. W. JACOBS
BECAUSE
HE LIKED IT

A DOG DAY

OR

THE ANGEL IN THE HOUSE

A.M.
7.0.
Woke up feeling rather below par, owing to disturbed rest. Hardly enough energy to stretch myself. In the middle of the night a strange man came in by the kitchen window, very quietly, with a bag. I chummed up to him at once. He was nice to me, and I was nice to him. He got me down a piece of meat that I could not reach myself. While I was engaged on this, he took a whole lot of silver things and put them into the bag. Then, as he was leaving, the brute—I believe, now, it was an accident—trod on my toe, making me yelp with pain. I bit him heartily, and he dropped his bag, and scurried off through the window again. My yelp-

ing soon woke up the whole house, and, in a very short time, old Mr. Brown and young Mr. Brown appear. They at once spot the bag of silver. They then declare I have saved the house, and make no end of fuss of me. I am a hero. Later on Miss Brown came down and fondled me lots, and kissed me, and tied a piece of pink ribbon round my neck, and made me look a fool. What's the good of ribbon, I should like to know? It's the most beastly tasting stuff there ever was.

8.30.   Ate breakfast with difficulty. Have no appetite.

8.35.   Ate kittens' breakfast.

8.36.   An affair with the cat (the kittens' mother). But I soon leave her, as the coward does not fight fair, using claws.

9.0.   Washed by Mary. A hateful business. Put into a tub, and rubbed all over—mouth, tail, and everywhere—with filthy soapy water, that loathsome cat looking on all the while, and sneering in her dashed superior way. I don't know, I am sure, why the hussy should be so conceited. She has to clean herself. I keep a servant to clean me. At the same time I often wish I was a black dog. They keep clean so much longer. Every finger-mark shows up so frightfully on the white part of me. I am a sight after Cook has been stroking me.

9.30.   Showed myself in my washed state to the family. All very nice to me. Quite a triumphal entry, in fact. It is simply wonderful the amount of kudos I've got from that incident with the man. Miss Brown (whom I rather like) particularly enthusiastic. Kissed me again and again, and called me " a dear, clean, brave, sweet-smelling little doggie."

9.40.   While a visitor was being let in at the front door I rushed out, and had the most glorious roll in the mud. Felt more like my old self then.

9.45.   Visited the family again. Shrieks of horror on seeing me caked in mud. But all agreed that I was not to be scolded to-day as I was a hero (over that man!). All, that is, except Aunt Brown, whose hand, for some reason or other, is always against me—though nothing is too good for the cat. She stigmatised me, quite gratuitously, as "a horrid fellow."

9.50.   Glorious thought!   Rushed upstairs
         and rolled over and over on the old
         maid's bed.   Thank Heaven, the mud
         was still wet!

10 to 10.15.   Wagged tail.

10.16.   Down into kitchen. While cook is watching regiment pass, I play with chops, and bite big bits out of them. Cook, who is quite upset for the day by seeing so many soldiers, continues to cook the chops without noticing.

10.20 to 1.0.   Dozed.

1.0   Ate dinner.

1.15.   Ate kittens' dinner.

1.20.   Attacked by beast of cat again. She scratched my hind-leg, and at that I refused to go on. Mem.: to take it out of her kittens later.

1.25.   Upstairs into dining-room. Family not finished lunch yet. Young Mr. Brown throws a bread pellet at me, hitting me on the nozzle. An insult. I swallow the insult. Then I go up to Miss Brown and look at her with my great pleading eyes. I guessed it: they are irresistible. She gives me a piece of pudding. Aunt Brown tells her she shouldn't. At which, with great pluck, Miss Brown tells her to mind her own business. I admire that girl more and more.

1.30.   A windfall. A whole dish of mayon-
naise fish on the slab in the hall. Before you can say Jack Robinson I have
bolted it.

1.32.   Curious pains in my underneath.

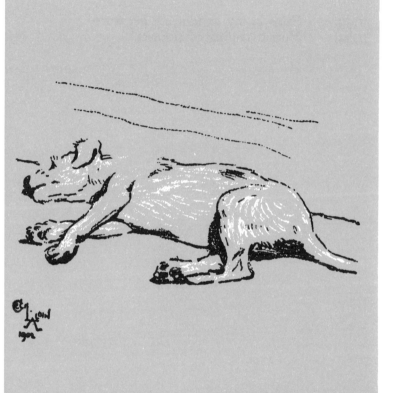

1.33.   Pains in my underneath get worse.
1.34.   Horrid feeling of sickness.

1.35.   Rush up into Aunt Brown's room, and am sick there.

1.37.   Better. Think I shall pull through if I am careful.

1.40.   Almost well again.

1.41.   Quite well again. Thank Heavens! It was a narrow shave that time. People ought not to leave such stuff about.

1.42.   Up into dining-room. And, to show how well I am, I gallumph round and round the room, at full pelt, about twenty times, steering myself by my tail. Then, as a grand finale, I jump twice on to the waistcoat-part of old Mr. Brown, who is sleeping peacefully in the armchair. He wakes up very angry indeed, and uses words I have never heard before. Even Miss Brown, to my no little surprise, says it is very naughty of me. Old Mr. Brown insists on my being punished, and orders Miss Brown to beat me. Miss Brown runs the burglar for all he is worth. But no good. Old Mr. Brown is dead to all decent feeling! So Miss Brown beats me. Very nice. Thoroughly en-

joyable. Just like being patted. But, of course, I yelp, and pretend it hurts frightfully, and do the sad eye business, and she soon leaves off and takes me into the next room and gives me six pieces of sugar. Good business. Must remember always to do this. Before leaving she kisses me and explains that I should not have jumped on poor Pa, as he is the man who goes to the City to earn bones for me. Something in that, perhaps. Nice girl.

2.0 to 3.15.   Attempt to kill fur rug in back
          room.   No good.
3.15 to 3.45.   Sulked.
3.46.   Small boy comes in and strokes me.
          I snap at him.   *I will not* be everyone's
          plaything.

3.47 to 4.0. Another attempt to kill rug. Would have done it this time, had not that odious Aunt Brown come in and interfered. I did not say anything, but gave her such a look, as much as to say, " I'll do for you one day." I think she understood.

4.0 to 5.15. Slept.

5.15.   Awakened by a bad attack of eczema.

5.20 to 5.30.   Slept again.
5.30.   Awakened again by eczema. Caught
       one.

5.30 to 6.0.   Frightened   canary   by   staring greedily at it.

6.0.   Visited kitchen-folk.   Boned some
bones.

6.15.   Stalked a kitten in kitchen-passage.
          The other little cowards ran away.
6.20.   Things are looking brighter: helped
          mouse escape from cat.

6.30.   Upstairs, past the drawing-room. Door of old Mrs. Brown's bedroom open invitingly. I entered. Never been in before. Nothing much worth having. Ate a few flowers out of a bonnet. Beastly.

Then into Miss Brown's room. Very tidy when I entered. Discovered there packet labelled " High-class Pure Confectionery." Not bad. Pretty room.

7.0. Down to supper. Ate it, but without much relish. I am off my feed to-day.

7.15. Ate kittens' supper. But I do wish they would not give them that eternal fish. I am getting sick of it.

7.16. Sick of it in the garden.

7.25. Nasty feeling of lassitude comes over me, with loss of all initiative, so I decide to take things quietly, and lie down by the kitchen fire. Sometimes I think that I am not the dog that I was.

8.0.   Hooray! Appetite returning.

8.1.   Ravenous.

8.2.   Have one of the nicest pieces of coal I have ever come across.

8.5.   Nose around the kitchen floor, and glean a bit of onion, an imitation tortoise-shell comb, a shrimp (almost entire), an abominably stale chunk of bread, and about half a yard of capital string. After coal, I think I like string best. The family have noticed what a lot of this I stow away, and it was not a bad idea of young Mr. Brown's, the other day, that, if I had the end of a piece of string always hanging from my mouth, they could use me as a string-box. Though it is scarcely a matter for joking about. Still, it made me laugh.

8.30.   If one had to rely on other people one might starve. Fortunately, in the hall I happen on the treacle-pudding, and I get first look in. Lap up the treacle, and leave the suet for the family. A1.

8.40.   Down into the kitchen again. Sit by the fire, and pretend I don't know what treacle is like. But that vile cat is there, and I believe she guesses—keeps looking round at me with her hateful superior look. Dash her, what right has she got to give herself such airs? She's not half my size, and pays no taxes. Dash her smugness. Dash her altogether. The sight of her maddens me—and, when her back is turned, I rush at her and bite her. The crafty coward wags her tail pretending she likes it, so I do it again, and then she rounds on me, and scratches my paw viciously, drawing blood, and making

me howl with pain.   This brings Miss
Brown down in a hurry.

She kisses me, tells the cat she is a
naughty cat (*I'd* have killed her for
it), gives me some sugar, and wraps the
paw up in a bread poultice, Lord, how
that girl loves me!

9.0.   Ate the bread poultice.
9.15.   Begin to get sleepy.
9.15 to 10.0.   Dozed.
10.0.   Led to kennel.
10.15.   Lights out. Thus ends another dernd
dull day.